DIGITAL DETOX

DIGITAL DETOX

Finding Balance in a Hyperconnected World

B. VINCENT

QuillQuest Publishers

CONTENTS

CHAPTER 1

Introduction

Welcome to the digital age. The advent and spread of digital technologies is having far-reaching and profound consequences for human society, on an unprecedented scale and at an unimaginable rate. Today, the internet connects more than half of humanity and is a tool for all information and communication. Over time and increasingly at present, it becomes an integral part of today's lifestyle, changing the experience of life and the way we relate to the world, to others, and ourselves. It is promoted from outside and from within, in interaction with social, psychological, cultural, biological, and ethical factors. The internet thus becomes a governing capital of the real world, it is its own world. The digital world has become an addictive vector and a predisposing cause of mental obsession and loss of meaning. Today, life invites all frustrated, unprogrammed, disoriented individuals to take place in a digital trap like nothing other than their own self-appealing demonic dreams.

The first chapter presents a general introduction to the topic, as it is appropriate in the context of a work focused on the consequences for human lives. The second chapter then presents a comprehensive summary of digital drugs and negative effects. The third chapter deals with the existing "detox methods". The fourth chapter summarizes various opinions and, as far as possible, statements about the possibility of mitigating the negative consequences of internet use for human lives and other issues that do not apply to their development. The fifth and final chapter examines my opinion.

1.1. The impact of technology on our lives

However, a darker side to this hyperconnectivity also exists because it has led to undesirable effects on our financial, emotional, social, and physical health. The average person checks their cellphone about 85 times a day, and adolescents can easily send an average of 100 text messages a day. The emailing culture has created a 24/7 work environment. Furthermore, it has exposed people to email and work-addiction symptoms as well as enhanced strains in people's work lives. Goals and overuse of digital leisure activities, including sexting, gambling, viewing online pornography, and gaming, have generated urgent public health concerns. The disrupting form of communication has led us down the path of multitasking during social interactions, contributing to further individual and family disconnection.

The advances we have made in communications technologies have drastically changed the way we live. The convenience of anytime, anywhere access to digital content and information has made life easier and more efficient for many people. For example, we can book an airline ticket, check in for a flight, upgrade our ticket, and then board a plane seamlessly using different apps that make life easier and richer. It is useful to remind ourselves daily of this richness and how the digital content keeps society hyperconnected. Even during our leisure time, we can be productive. For instance, access to email, texting, and social media communication permit us to instantaneously connect with people in our social circles, allowing us to effectively multitask during social interactions or even when we leisurely relax.

1.2. The need for a digital detox

Modern technology has extended our working hours and made employers expect a faster response to work-related problems, usually answered over email. One in four US workers report checking their work email constantly during non-business hours, while 50% admit to checking it while outside standard work hours. Damage is caused to employees' health from the stress of being constantly connected to work when you're supposed to be resting, exercising, cooking, playing with children, or considering other non-work related tasks. Conversely, research shows a correlation between unplugging from work and improved wellbeing. In a study on work connectivity and its relatedness to work and non-work stress, the lead author recommended that creating an off-hours culture in the workplace, within an organization, is vital to reclaiming necessary time away from work to connect with family, de-stress, and focus on one's well-being.

Waiting tables soon became an afterthought, a sort of menial step on the way to higher aspirations. Despite new types of technology, it remained a reliable job for college students, a place to bond with peers, and an occasional distraction from the more pressing matters of schoolwork. I was able to maintain a healthy work-life balance, mainly because once I clocked out, I was free to break away from the world of work. There was no carryover from the restaurant since we didn't have company cell phones or we weren't encouraged to check our emails frequently. I could focus on my midterm or final exam schedule and plan how to tackle my responsibilities. Similar to the waitressing atmosphere, other retail and fast-food jobs generally don't expect their employees to take on extra work or be constantly tethered to work. On the contrary, the working world is significantly more accessible to employees due to smartphones and other mobile technology that can connect anyone to work-related issues at any time of the day.

CHAPTER 2

Benefits of a digital detox

The benefits include the number of hours reduced in front of the screen, which increased engagement with live tasks. This also means less TV watching and interacting with friends and families, as well as reading, increased. Expert clinical psychologist Elizabeth Cohen in New York showed that severe gamers aged between 10 and 17 years old had improved interpersonal behavior and depression. A digital detox at work may improve morale, improve team skills, and improve company profits. So seriously, that digital detox camps are being implemented in schools globally. Schools have incorporated digital detox because it was discovered that 58% of children aged between 3 and 16 years old were online. 60% of these children were between 10 and 15 years old; hence, one of the causes of these children's decline in sleep, schoolwork, and emotional stability. A report by Ohio State University highlighted that users with narcissistic behaviors and low self-esteem may upload the number of posts, which may lead to regret if low self-esteem individuals upload posts that were meant to be surgical but are offensive.

A 2017 research suggests that tech detoxing can reduce the level of stress and anxiety felt by employees. As well, in 2019, the theft of cryptocurrency rose by 400%, and it is often advertised on social media; therefore, taking a step back may reduce the chance of falling victim to scammers. An internet and gaming addiction treatment service for young individuals showed that 6 out of 10 children (6–18 years old) spent 20+ hours a week on online or computer games. They mentioned that the reduction in screen time aids their mental and physical health; for example, better sleep, improved self-esteem, and good overall behavior. In 2015, a 5-day tech break in children may mitigate the negative effects of heavy technology use, which includes poor posture, screen addiction, and internet overuse. An interview with a tech 'addict' mentioned that his senses have dulled, and by turning off his phone, he can enjoy the subtleties and natural beauty around him. Courts in Wales have trialed a tech-free day in court. Their aim is to encourage the younger generation to have a tech detox, some hours or days, in the case of trials. This not only improved the performance in courts, and research has also shown that efficient multitasking encourages the individual to be more productive.

2.1. Improved mental health and well-being

Some researchers have tried to translate them into an optimal email schedule for the well-being of employees. Nilofer Merchant concluded that in ten years or more access to areas of research, problems such as excessive email recognition or just endless email appointments come at discounted prices from our mental and psychological health. We need disconnection times for personal and mental health. Experiments suggested contained transaction management, where one would have email messages, notifications, and other digital tools at regular intervals. This would help reduce our perception from the moment, the rush fee, but still have a regular, comprehensive conversation.

When it comes to well-being, the effect of connecting to the digital world is the ability to both remain connected while separating from the stress of awareness from our day-to-day lives. Research findings are consistent as they are conclusions, involving thousands of adults and psychologists, that the use of casual electronics can cause unhealthy amounts of stress, and therefore significant emotional and physical health risks. A single study focuses on how constant computer sessions or occasional e-mail updates can change our work-related stress levels and it is recommended that we need a detox period revitalization from computers. The National Study of Stress and Bullying Work provides similar results. Corporations appear to remain in the world completely. In the working area before they have received an email, the recipients stepped into emails, gave them time or lung pressure.

2.2. Increased productivity and focus

From an employer's perspective, increased productivity of workers and reduced costs may act in favor of supporting lean digital media diets and regular digital detoxes. Reduced usage could also lead to improvements in quality of both communication and collaboration. Widespread adoption would be even stronger if the entire leadership were visible champions of digital detox themselves. This could be in the form of no-communication timeframes and "detox days". High-pressure jobs are less likely to benefit from a lean media diet, with possible small improvements when the digital detox becomes regular. Put in another way, non-managers benefit more from regular detoxing than leaders do. However, leaders' value as role models can surely not be underestimated as they can inspire a more widespread adoption of detox practices. Finally, although few groups will benefit from high digital detox-related improvements, for most users digital detoxing brings about moderate to large advantages.

Cutting distractions and stress can open the door to better work performance for employees. When workers are stressed, their productivity decreases. Workers become less able to focus and concentrate, and increased use of social media can also eat into productivity levels. Despite its digital connotation, the term "digital detox" is more about eliminating the chronic impact of a mobile and hyper-connected world, where information overload (whether personal or job-related) substantially impairs one's ability to truly relax, focus, and think deeply. A variety of studies have linked information overload and constant work interruptions with negative effects on cognitive performance and stress, as well as the need to recover both physically and psychologically. Conversely, a lean media diet (i.e., lower usage) goes hand-in-hand with performance, work/life balance, and improved general well-being. This suggests that strategies for a regular "detox" from digital communications can have a major impact on levels of creativity and our ability to come up with original solutions to workplace problems.

2.3. Better sleep quality

A study in Japan showed that adolescents who increased their use of smartphones or watching TV for 5 hours or more had concomitant attention deficit. When they decrease time using these devices, they show a reduction in the impact, as well as the severity of symptoms by 88% and 64% respectively.

According to Taiwanese research, an increase in daily screentime for 2-5-year-olds was associated not only with significantly increased sedentary time (e.g. video time) but also with aggravated ADHD symptoms and poor motor skills. On the other hand, children who have strictly adhered to screen time recommendations show a slower advancement of suboptimal attention behaviors and reduced overall psychopathological problems. Keep in mind that children who have been watching a screen for at least two and a half hours a day for 18 months had significantly lower inferior frontal cortex levels.

Swiss researchers monitored the daily screen time and sleep duration and compared the results to find out the direct connection. Perhaps the most striking discovery is the use of digital media. When the media use was passive, sleep duration suffered by the worst of the 6-7-year-old children. Teens lasted the least sleep while watching TV, while the toddlers slept the fewest hours if they watched videos or DVDs.

Recent studies indicate that the presence of "interactive screen-time" (the type of activity more frequent amongst digital device users) is significantly associated with longer sleep latencies and shorter sleep duration. These results suggest similar associations involved when examining interactive screen/activity use and poor sleep hygiene indicators. Not only does screentime late into the evenings detract, but screen time during the day and conditions in general affect the quality of sleep.

CHAPTER 3

Strategies for a successful digital detox

Unlike sugar detoxing or going teetotal, a total digital detox is often not feasible because of the ways in which we are entangled with digital technologies. We rely on smartphones, email and other digital tools in our workplace and for personal planning and communication. There is always some need to be accessible. But most of us also have developed compulsive habits associated with being easily distracted by notifications, monitoring social media in downtime, or simply enjoying opportunities to browse news, gossip, opinion and entertainment sites. I think this is particularly surprising: that even though we are experiencing exhaustion and withdrawal effects associated with the use of digital technologies, which are keeping us from experiencing the real world and each other, our inclination is often to do more of it and look for our enjoyment and relaxation there. I hypothesize that our very effort to balance our digital lives with our offline world is compounding the problem of addiction and making the ultimate elusive goal of balance harder to achieve.

Digital detoxing is not about rejecting technology or the digital world outright. It is about finding some balance, negotiating a medium between the digital and non-digital world that best suits our values and where possible, that best aligns our behaviour with how we wish to live. A majority of the 100 participants in my research said they would like to reduce their reliance on electronic devices and reported wanting to experience more of the natural world and more 'real life' interactions. Many of the participants also struggled with feeling overwhelmed or unwell because of the ways in which they were using technology. Most heartening, however, was the fact that a large majority (81%) believe a balance can be struck between life online and life offline.

3.1. Setting clear boundaries and goals

If you want to gather some motivation and learn more about setting and breaking habits in general, we suggest checking out the Charles Duhigg book called "The Power of Habit: Why We Do What We Do in Life and Business." It can help you identify where all your energy goes. Schedule personal time also for your digital world because habits are formed in about 21 days, and it's important for your online behavior to have a positive connotation and personal value. Even if you missed a couple of scheduled times, remember any effort makes a difference, and as a habit-building, it's all about the routine, don't give up! Regular times on your calendar could mean meditating, doing a sport, spending time with family, or even organizing your calendar or putting in place a new system to help you develop good habits.

Understanding your online behavior is a good first step in establishing clear boundaries and goals. It's worth highlighting the "Keep it Simple" principle of the KISS Movement. Setting up good structural habits in your online habits that will allow you digital resilience, such as having digital duties. For example, if you're working on a project or assignment and a non-urgent message comes in, save the message, finish your work, and then take a scheduled break to see what new messages arrived. You can even schedule this time. Obviously, different kinds of working environments come with different responsibilities, but in any case, it's good to have guidelines that respect your time and your private space. If you've established your working hours, the first and last working hour should only be about focusing on the day ahead or what has been achieved during the day.

3.2. Engaging in offline activities

3.3. Engaging with media mindfully. Participants facilitated the notion of consuming media more selectively as a way of disengaging from digital devices. Common themes highlighted included recipes for cooking, gardening, reading, and art. These activities were perceived to promote learning, creativity, and the sharing of ideas among participants. Moreover, individuals described that taking on a device-free day would allow them to spend time "on the things that matter." Serial media usage during leisure time was described as detrimental to general personal satisfaction and emotional fulfillment. However, some participants expressed that they valued conversations that could occur as a means of socialization through social media, instant messaging, or online forums. In the context of remote communities, engaging in online social activities was described as a way of ceasing feelings of isolation. Respondents referred to video calls or chats that provided an inconspicuous means of communicating with loved ones.

3.2. Engaging in offline activities. Finding enjoyment in offline activities was perceived to be a way of disengaging from the digital realm. Hobbies, in particular, were viewed as being especially beneficial, allowing respondents to maintain focus and expressing a sense of personal satisfaction. Gardening, playing an instrument, painting, or spending time in nature were highlighted as offline activities that permitted moments of solitude and calm: "Great way of unplugging, focus on music, using brainpower while doing something enjoyable." This sentiment was reinforced by participants who explained that engaging in offline activities allowed for the development of meaningful emotional connections with others: spending time with family, visiting loved ones, or hosting a dinner with friends. Those respondents who engaged in offline work described that this could foster focus and allow for a winding down of digital engagement.

3.3. Practicing mindfulness and self-reflection

The challenge immediately became clear as I forced my eyelids open for the first time. I was sharing a zen-dorm open space room with approximately 18 other women and one open ventilation concept in the ceiling to help maintain airflow. The alarm was my signal that I should exit the room while it was still dark, since that hour was reserved for meditation only. Rolling over and reaching for my unassuming iPhone, the urge to dismiss it is strong, but I held myself accountable to my word. I turned the phone off and the lights overhead on, softly slipping in and out of my bunk bed to quickly dress so my hot morning tea was waiting for me downstairs. After two sixty-minute sessions of deep meditation, a ninety-minute yoga session with one of the greatest yogis of the retreat, Charley Castex, and breakfast, I found myself upstairs getting ready to take some of the time towards my "new pledge." Not even an hour into my 24-hour fast, the craving to use my phone to write and take pictures of the beautiful monastery was there, and Paco was definitely not having it.

Before leaving for the retreat, each of us took an "iBreak" card. We were asked to write down an amount of time - anywhere from half an hour to half a day - that we pledged to spend without the use of technology over the digital detox. Pledging to take the time to disconnect, think, and be more mindful sounded like a simple enough proposition. I decided that I would give up technology for a full 24 hours. That will allow me to be truly present, but at the same time it would also be a bit of a stretch. Aside from not using my phone, I was also pledging to ban computer use, which I needed for my writing. I had a feeling that my resolution was one of the more extreme, but no one else seemed fazed. Fast forward to the first day of silent retreat, I woke at 6:00 a.m. to three alarm rings.

3.4. Establishing a support system

Social networks can bring us together in the digital world. On the internet, we may find others who we can connect with while discussing our struggles, interests, or ideas. We can also shop, order food, navigate using GPS, check sports updates and news, make dinner reservations, request Ubers, and even engage in online activities such as watching movies, TV, or YouTube videos. However, to elevate the relationships in our life, it is important to be present with our loved ones, focus our attention on them, and enhance the quality of moments by involving others in our life experiences. Research suggests the importance of creating experiences that evoke joy and help us connect in the present with our companions to foster positive affects and deep connections.

One of the strategies I found for managing low-level anxiety is to talk about it. Doing a PhD, I feel intense pressure to be perfect in my productivity, even at nights and weekends. Being unable to turn off my brain and relax makes me feel like a failure. I discovered I could alleviate some of these problems by talking with someone, like a friend or my outplacement coach, about my struggles. My outlook changed, I was able to accept the reality as it was, relax my pace, and accept the notion that I am doing my best. I also found calm in exercising in the outdoors. Running in the woods reminded me that I should focus on how I feel in the moment instead of what a watch says is an appropriate pace. By feeling accomplished instead of anxious, I was able to embrace the moment for what it was.

CHAPTER 4

Maintaining balance in a hyperconnected world

Tips for maintaining a balance include having a 'device hiatus', taking a digital step back, and understanding that we all need time to think, ideate, and innovate—time where we are not being bombarded by multiple messages and emails. By far the hardest aspect to manage is how digital transformation and constant connectivity are changing the nature of connectedness itself. Employees still maintain that connection—albeit a virtual one—with their immediate work teams, but the nature of connectedness with other design and manufacturing professionals has certainly changed with this network of virtual relationships. To allay specific connectivity concerns, companies need to ensure employees have access to role model behavior and are offered intervention strategies. Once employees understand the scale of the risk to their collective work-life balance and health, they can begin to make changes and ask for the right system of support.

A combination of current events and the role I inhabit at my primary place of employment has got me thinking about the impact of the 'digital fatigue' we all experience on a daily basis. Some days, I feel connected to everyone with a device, but isolated from the people closest to me. In a hyperconnected world, devices allow us to be more productive, more efficient, and more effective; however, if not managed correctly, they can become productivity black holes. In his book Enlightenment Now, Steven Pinker discusses two types of 'fatigue', one physical and the other virtual aka digital. Pinker states that the amount of information available can either be stimulating or distressing depending on how effectively and frequently we can disconnect. While disconnection remains a personal responsibility, the impact of virtual fatigue—on individuals as well as corporate health—cannot be ignored. Disconnection from virtual work is not merely a requirement but is essential for a healthy work-life balance.

By Rini Das

Digital Detox: Finding Balance in a Hyperconnected World

4.1. Creating healthy technology habits

If everything goes well, we immediately passionately react to simple, old-style extensions. We hope that someone will absolutely log into it and beg us to hesitantly close. But that never happens, so we're bold. We'll do it alone! Then, we wonder where the difference between the synchronization of our connection to these insidious little submarines and soybeans (our products?) is and when old good fashion privacy may also need to be suspended. public space. Countless emails and personal scheduling messages may now pass a visual inspection if you enter an open 24-hour fast-food office, and they are regularly sent, rather secretly, to the silent (at least for the other party) sanctuaries like all others. ridiculous literature.

We need a lifestyle that is moderate in all things, including digital consumption and selection. Sure, you can miss out if you only limit yourself to email and use it only at home. The danger described is what some experts call overuse, because we do not use technology in moderation, from simple SMS text messages to email and GPS, digital equipment to the entire internet. Many people today find it difficult to evade the siren call of email or computer games or experience the empty gap. At work, we open the Outlook software as soon as we arrive (or before!) and hope that there may be urgent new messages that will give us a direction for this day. If there are no more messages, we see something is wrong: the boss or the colleagues are tapping me on the fingers, even on Sabbath! If we have some free time during our home program, we quickly sit at the computer to play this fascinating new game just waiting to be started, we can't wait to play a new campaign.

4.2. Setting realistic expectations

How long technology is used does matter, but less so than the negative exchanges or poor sleep associated with technology use. It is worth noting the recommended time limit of one hour of use or less is likely a reasonable goal for educational technology use as well. Given the known benefits of education, and learning technology use on oral communications and writing or literacy use for all ages, it is reasonable to desire the social benefits available to many technology users on social media. Users should be aware of symptoms associated with increasing technology use as well as the potential issues associated with sharing personal information on the social media sites they use. Furthermore, it's probably safe to say that all social media users know they may exhibit some level of social exclusion when they use the sites. According to the bitrate, on average, users have 310 friends, but in their minds, they feel they can only trust four of those people.

Studies continue to show that using social media can be harmful to mental health. Although two-thirds of Facebook users exhibit symptoms of "technostress," only 5% of users were able to limit their use of the site. If, as we've mentioned, it's difficult to resist engaging with technology, then even fewer users are probably willing or able to cut back on their use. Considering the mixed findings of previous studies, and findings from my research and others, do you believe that setting realistic goals around the use of social media and technology, rather than setting an all-or-nothing guideline about avoiding social media, ultimately provides the best strategy for using social media? In other words, forgo the digital detox and instead set a limit, determining at what levels use of technology is functional or dysfunctional. Using social media for one hour per day—or less— may allow you to mitigate the potential harm of technology use and enhance social connectedness.

4.3. Finding alternative ways to stay connected

The main thing is to remember that in digital detox, what is really important is not to eliminate technologies strictly, but to find a balance in the use of them so that they do not invade and be a barrier to our social interactions and can also help us improve our relationships with what is most important to satisfy our need for social support. In this situation, as experts also warn, the idea is to find a natural and healthy use of these technologies that accompanies everything humans need in life and that digital detox can be a style of private and public life. Many times we believe that these guidelines are limited to the domestic sphere and in any situation, we confuse undervaluation and give us a single continuity digital treatment because this oscillation silhouette how we intend to change, and the efforts that we put into it.

In reality, many of us find it quite natural to keep contact with sounds instead of personal conversations for the feelings of fellowship and coherence that are strengthened by social support. Something similar is happening with digital detox. There is a large part of the population that still does not find the danger of being always hyperconnected. Being hyperconnected is accepted as a normal state of postmodern society. Therefore, we need to reflect and demonstrate that leisure alternatives not mediated by ICT can also generate those same feelings that are strengthened by social support. In this sense, it is essential to promote personal contact alternatives, to develop social skills and to know that there are also alternative forms of leisure other than digital ones. Some time ago, people played in family, not every man in his cell phone. If we simplify family communication we will also contribute to less social support and to less perceived happiness.